GW00372770

www.booksbyboxer.com

Published by
Books By Boxer, Leeds, LS13 4BS UK
Books by Boxer (EU), Dublin D02 P593 IRELAND
© Books By Boxer 2021
All Rights Reserved
**MADE IN MALTA**

ISBN: 9781909732834

THE GAME OF GOLF WAS FIRST OFFICIALLY DOCUMENTED IN THE YEAR 1457 IN SCOTLAND.

IN A 1457 ACT OF THE SCOTTISH PARLIAMENT, THE GAMES OF 'GOWF' AND 'FUTBALL' WERE PROHIBITED IN AN EDICT FROM KING JAMES II OF SCOTLAND TO LIMIT DISTRACTIONS TO THE PRACTICE OF ARCHERY WHICH HAD MILITARY PURPOSE.

The rule states the prohibition of: "obtaining, holding or using membership cards for gyms, clubs, golf clubs, or various other types of consumer cards, or entering private clubs".

Since 1891 and set by St. Andrews Golf Club (the governing golf body at the time), all golf holes must be 10.8cm wide.

The first hole cutter was invented and used by the Royal Musselbrough Golf Club who used a drainage pipe, which happened to be exactly 10.8cm wide.

## JAMES II OF SCOTLAND

Born: 16th October 1430
Coronation: 25th March 1437
Died: 3rd August 1460

Cause of death: Hit by an exploding canon during a siege of Roxburgh Castle in 1460.

THE FIRST KNOWN TOURNAMENT OF WOMEN'S GOLF WAS PLAYED ON 9TH JANUARY 1811, HELD AT MUSSELBURGH IN SCOTLAND IN WHICH THE TOWN'S FISHWIVES PLAYED AGAINST EACH OTHER.

WOMEN'S GOLF SOCIETIES HOWEVER WERE NOT OFFICIALLY FORMED UNTIL THE LATER HALF OF THE 19TH CENTURY.

Mussleburgh golf club has records dating back to 1672, although reported Mary Queen of Scots played golf in Musselburgh as early as 1567.

In 2009 the Guinness World Records named Musselburgh as the World's oldest golf course, however the title was revoked and is now held by St. Andrews when records were found dating 1552.

GOLF IS ONE OF THE ONLY SPORTS THAT HAS EVER BEEN PLAYED ON THE MOON, THE OTHER BEING JAVELIN!

ALAN SHEPARD, COMMANDER OF NASA'S APOLLO 14 MISSION, FAMOUSLY TOOK TWO SHOTS ON THE MOON ON THE 6TH FEBRUARY 1971. SHEPARD FOLLOWED THE SECOND SHOT BY TELLING THE CAMERA THE BALL WENT FOR 'MILES AND MILES.'

# ALAN SHEPARD

**Born:** 18th November 1923
**Died:** 21st July 1998
**Space missions:** Apollo 14, Mercury-Redstone 3

Alan Shepard was the 5th Man to walk on the moon,
and the first American to travel into space in 1961,
a decade prior.

TIGER WOODS MADE HIS FIRST
HOLE-IN-ONE AT ONLY EIGHT YEARS
OLD, AT HEARTWELL GOLF COURSE
IN LONG BEACH, CALIFORNIA.

ADDITIONALLY, WOODS WAS THE
YOUNGEST PLAYER TO HAVE A
CAREER GRAND SLAM, HAVING WON
ALL FOUR PROFESSIONAL MAJOR
CHAMPIONSHIPS.

# TIGER WOODS

**Full name:** Eldrick Tont Woods
**Born:** 30 December 1975

Woods has earned the most during his career so far
than any other player in PGA tour history.

THERE'S A 12,500 TO 1 CHANCE OF MAKING A HOLE-IN-ONE, WITH THE ODDS DROPPING TO 2,500 TO 1 FOR PROFESSIONAL GOLFERS.

AT THE 1989 U.S. OPEN, FOUR PROS ACED THE SAME HOLE (NO. 6) DURING THE SAME ROUND (SECOND). ODDS: 1.6 MILLION TO 1.

Odds of an amateur making a hole-in-one:
12,500 to 1
Odds of a low-handicapper making a hole-in-one:
5,000 to 1
Odds of a professional golfer making an ace:
2,500 to 1
Odds for an average golfer on a 200-yard par-3:
150,000 to 1

Golf balls were originally made out of wood until the seventeenth century, when the 'feathery' golf ball was invented.

A 'feathery' golf ball was a leather outer stuffed with boiled goose feathers that was stitched up and painted. The balls were made while the leather and feathers were still wet so that the leather shrunk while drying and the feathers inside expanded to create a hardened ball.

Each 'feathery' ball required a bucket full of boiled goose feathers and the cost of a 'feathery' ball could often be higher than the price of a club! Not only was the 'feathery' ball expensive it was delicate and could only last 2 rounds of golf or could completely come apart when wet.

IN 2015 THE CHINESE COMMUNIST PARTY BANNED ALL 88 MILLION OF IT'S MEMBERS FROM JOINING GOLF CLUBS.

CHINA HAS ALSO STRICTLY CONTROLLED THE AMOUNT OF GOLF COURSES BEING BUILT IN THE COUNTRY, WITH THE NUMBER OF COURSES ALLOWED FLUCTUATING IN RECENT YEARS.

The first hole cutter invented in 1829 still exists and is on display at the club.

Lightning has struck American Golfer Lee Trevino – twice! One of those times was at the Western Open, near Chicago in 1975. Trevino suffered injuries to his spine, which resulted in him needing surgery.

Following being struck by lightning, Trevino famously replied to a reporter after asking what he would do if it began to storm again, he stated that he would take out his 1-iron and point it to the sky, "because not even God can hit a 1-iron."

## Lee Buck Trevino

Nickname: The Merry Mex, Supermex
Born: December 1, 1939
Professional wins: 92

A GOLF BALL ON AVERAGE HAS BETWEEN 380 AND 460 DIMPLES, DEPENDING ON THE BALL'S MAKE. THE DIMPLE DEPTH IS ALSO HIGHLY CONTROLLED, AS A SLIGHT VARIANCE IN THIS CAN CAUSE A SIGNIFICANT DIFFERENCE IN HOW THE BALL FLIES

IF GOLF BALLS WERE SMOOTH THEY WOULD ONLY BE ABLE TO TRAVEL ABOUT HALF AS FAR AS THE DIMPLED BALL WE KNOW.

Golf ball manufacturer Titleist discovered and have since put in much research into the aerodynamics behind how dimples affect the speed of the ball.

23% OF ALL GOLFERS ARE WOMEN, WITH THE PERCENTAGE OF FEMALE REPRESENTATION RISING TO 31% IN BEGINNER GOLF.

MARY QUEEN OF SCOTS IS THOUGHT TO BE ONE THE FIRST FEMALE GOLFERS TO REGULARLY PLAY; FAMOUSLY RUMOURED THAT SHE WAS SEEN PLAYING GOLF WITHIN DAYS OF HER HUSBAND'S MURDER, WHICH FUELLED SPECULATION SHE WAS INVOLVED IN THE ASSASSINATION PLOT.

# MARY QUEEN OF SCOTS

**Born:** 8th December 1542
**Coronation:** 9th September 1543
**Died:** 8th February 1587

**Cause of death:** Beheaded, after being found guilty of plotting to assassinate Queen Elizabeth I of England.

Before golf tees were invented, golfers used mounds of sand to tee up balls! Using sand mounds was messy, so golfers were provided with towels and water to wash their hands.

To stop golfers and their caddies from taking sand from the hole, many courses provided sand boxes. Many of which are still in place in old courses today, however these now store fertilised soil for filling in divots.

The first commercial tee was invented in 1921 by American William Lowell. Known as the 'Reddy Tee' it was first manufactured in wood with a painted red top so it could be easily spotted.

BABE ZAHARIAS IS THE ONLY FEMALE TO HAVE MADE IT IN A MALE PGA TOUR EVENT.

REGARDED AS ONE OF THE GREATEST ATHLETES OF ALL TIME, SHE NOT ONLY WON 10 LGPA MAJOR CHAMPIONSHIPS IN HER CAREER BUT ALSO WON TWO GOLD MEDALS FOR TRACK AND FIELD AT THE 1932 SUMMER OLYMPICS. SHE ALSO ACTIVELY COMPETED IN BASKETBALL AND BASEBALL, HOLDING THE RECORD FOR THE FURTHEST BASEBALL THROW BY A WOMAN.

## FULL NAME: MILDRED ELLA DIDRIKSON ZAHARIAS

Nickname: Babe
Born: June 26th 1911
Died: September 27th 1956

Zaharias was inducted into the LPGA Hall of Fame in
1951 and further received the Bob Jones Award, the
highest honour given by the United States Golf
Association, posthumously 4 months after her death.

AS OF 2019, THERE ARE OVER 38,864 GOLF COURSES IN THE WORLD. ALMOST HALF OF THESE (AN EST. 16,752 COURSES), ARE IN THE USA ALONE.

England has the highest number of golf courses in Europe, home to 2270 courses, which is equivelent to 31620 holes.

Issette Miller (formally Pearson) was the founder of the LGU and a key developer in the universal handicap system.

Her system accounted for the experience and different abilities of the competitors.

Issette even has a trophy named after her; the Pearson Trophy was first awarded in 1910 and is now housed in the British Golf Museum in St. Andrews.

Golf was banned three separate times due to the Scottish government believing it interfered with military training between 1457 and 1744!

Football was also banned during this time for the same reason!

THE FIRST EVER BRITISH OPEN
CHAMPIONSHIP WAS HELD ON THE
17TH OCTOBER, 1860 AT PRESTWICK
GOLF CLUB IN SCOTLAND AND IS THE
OLDEST TOURNAMENT IN THE WORLD.

THE TOURNAMENT CONSISTED OF
3 ROUNDS OF THE 12 HOLE COURSE.

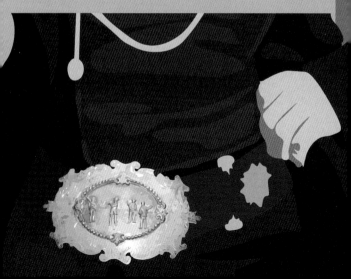

Most golfers at this time made their living from paying for bets as well as ball and club making, however the Open Championship offered the winner to receive the Challenge Belt, which was made from red leather with a silver buckle estimated at around £25.00, which nowadays would equate to just over £3000.00.

In 1975, Cosby Orr broke the world record as youngest golfer to shoot a hole-in-one at just five years old in Littleton, Colorado!

Golfer Phil Mickelson is naturally right handed, yet left handed when swinging golf clubs! This stems from him learning golf by mirroring his right-handed father's swing.

Full name: Philip Alfred Mickelson
Nickname: Lefty
Born: June 16th 1970

With his win at the 2021 PGA Championship, Mickelson became the oldest major championship winner in history at the age of 50 years, 11 months and 7 days old.

Joining a long list of US presidents who love to play golf, US President Woodrow Wilson took his hobby to the next level and had golf balls painted black, so he could play on the White House lawn during snow.

Wilson credits the game as a stress reliever for him during World War I, of which he served in office for the entirety.

# US President Woodrow Wilson

In office: March 4th 1913 - March 4th 1921
Born: December 28, 1856
Died: February 3rd 1924 (aged 67)

Won the Nobel Peach Prize in 1919 for his work as the leading power behind the League of Nations and ensuring world peace following the aftermath of the First World War.

For a number of reasons, playing golf on warmer days helps your golf balls travel further! Firstly, cold air is more dense than warm air so the ball will experience more friction and drag as it travels.

Secondly, the transfer of energy between ball and club is not as efficient which reduces speed, and finally the rubber materials used in our modern day golf balls respond better to warmer temperatures giving more velocity and spin.

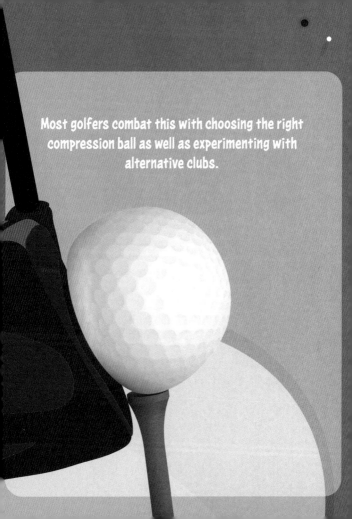

Most golfers combat this with choosing the right compression ball as well as experimenting with alternative clubs.

When in operation, the highest golf course in the world was Tactu Golf Club in Peru, sitting 14,335 ft. above sea level.

Known to have caused nosebleeds among golfers due to the elevation, the course closed in the mid-1990s and the land, that is owned by a mining company, is now overgrown with weeds and grasses.

In contrast, the lowest elevation golf course is the Furnace Creek Golf Course at Death Valley, California, at 214 feet below sea level.

CELINE DION ISN'T JUST A FAMOUS SINGER, SHE IS ALSO A SELF PROCLAIMED GOLF FANATIC. SO MUCH SO, SHE EVEN PREVIOUSLY OWNED LE MIRAGE GOLF CLUB IN QUEBEC!

PURCHASING THE COURSE AT THE END OF THE 1990S, THE SINGER IS REPUTED TO HAVE PAID OVER 15 MILLION CANADIAN DOLLARS.

Celine Dion boasts a handicap of 17 and her home features a semi-private course.

When playing golf with William. P. Smith and George. A. Crump, Ab. Smith coined the term 'birdie' in 1889, when he hit the ball just outside of the hole and claimed that it was a 'bird of a shot'.

In early 20th century slang, the term 'bird' meant excellent.

Other golfing terms that use birds include an 'Eagle' and an 'Albatross'.

Reknowned Mark Lye & Lee Trevino made an appearance in the 1996 film, Happy Gilmore, directed by Dennis Dugan.

The film follows Adam Sandler playing character Happy Gilmore, a rejected hockey player who applies his skills to the golf course to save his grandmother's house

In 2021, 25 years since the film was released, actors Adam Sandler and Christopher McDonald who played Gilmore's nemesis, recreated their famed shots on social media.

IF YOU WALKED THE DISTANCE
BETWEEN ALL 18 HOLES, YOU'D WALK
APPROXIMATELY FOUR MILES!

Last Hole
4 Miles

Actor Samuel L. Jackson loves golf so much that his contract states he must play golf twice a week when filming movies!

Jackson's handicap was an impressive 6.9 as of 2019 and is reputed to have shot a 78 while playing with Tiger Woods at St. Andrews. He also made an eagle on Augusta National's par-5 15th.

Samuel. L. Jackson started playing golf when tricked into coming to a driving range with his friends.

DOUG FORD NOT ONLY CORRECTLY PREDICTED HIS VICTORY, BUT ALSO HIS WINNING SCORE OF 283 BEFORE HE PLAYED THE 1957 MASTERS!

Full name: Douglas Michael Ford Sr.

Born: August 6th 1922
Died: May 14th 2018
Professional wins: 34

World Golf Hall of Fame: 2011
PGA Player of the Year: 1955

DURING WORLD WAR II IN 1942,
AUGUSTA NATIONAL GOLF CLUB
CLOSED FOR THREE YEARS TO RAISE
CATTLE AND TURKEY ON THE
CLUB'S GROUNDS.

Bobby Jones, Augusta National co-founder, had the idea of raising cattle on the course in order to keep the grass maintained and then later sell them for beef.

THE DON MUEANG
INTERNATIONAL AIRPORT IN
THAILAND HAS A GOLF COURSE IN
THE MIDDLE OF THE RUNWAY!

The Kantarat Golf Course in Bangkok allows golfers to tee off as close as 20 yards to passenger aeroplanes in a narrow strip between arriving and departing planes.

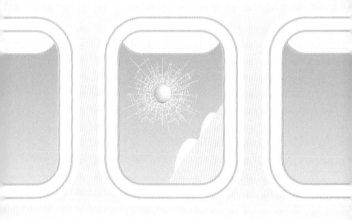

125,000 GOLF BALLS ARE SUNK IN THE 17TH HOLE WATER HAZARD AT THE TPC SAWGRASS COURSE!

The average time a used golf ball sits in the water is about 3-5 months before being retrieved.

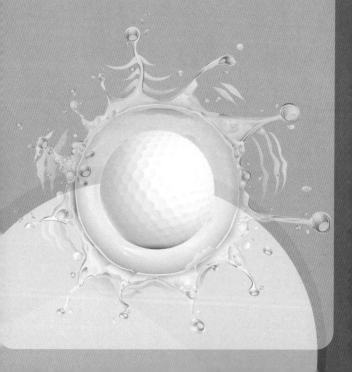

THE WORD CADDY ORIGINATES FROM THE FRENCH WORD CADET, MEANING YOUNGEST CHILD. THE TERM BECAME COMMON IN THE 18TH CENTURY AND WAS USED FOR A GENERAL PURPOSE ERRAND BOY IN SCOTTISH TOWNS.

IT WAS NOT UNTIL 1857 THAT THE DICTIONARY ATTRIBUTED THE TERM TO A PERSON MAINLY CARRYING GOLF CLUBS.

One of the first named caddies was Andrew Dickinson who as a child in 1681 acted as a fore-caddie for the Duke of York.

YOU'RE MORE LIKELY TO GET HIT BY LIGHTNING THAN MAKE TWO HOLE-IN-ONES IN A SINGLE ROUND.

THREE PROFESSIONAL GOLFERS HAVE ACHIEVED THIS FEAT ON THE SAME ROUND: BILL WHEDON IN 1955, YUSAKU MIYAZATO IN 2006 AND BRIAN HARMAN IN 2015.

In the 2020 Wyndham Championship, Si Woo Kim came close to becoming the fourth ever player to have two hole-in-ones in one round, however settled on one ace and a tap in birdie.

Chuiwan was a game in ancient China with some similarities to modern golf.

Played with a stick and ball, a book from the Song Dynasty (1050-1100) describes a game where a hole is dug into the ground with the aim to drive a ball into it.

The rules are very similar to modern golf, with a restricted number of clubs and terrains of varying difficulty.

TIGER WOODS HAS A SUPERSTITION
(REPUTED TO HAVE BEEN PASSED
DOWN FROM HIS MOTHER), THAT HE
ALWAYS WEARS A RED SHIRT ON THE
FINAL ROUND/DAY OF A
TOURNAMENT, AS RED REPRESENTS
POWER AND SUCCESS.

Red is a strange choice of colour as a red tee is considered unlucky by most golfers!

THE MASTERS CHAMPION DINNER IS HELD EACH YEAR ON THE TUESDAY OF MASTERS WEEK.

HOSTED BY THE PREVIOUS YEAR'S WINNER, THE DINNER IS ONLY OPEN TO WINNERS OF THE MASTERS.

The menu is decided by the host and has included food from all over the world in homage to each international players heritage.

La Jenny golf course in France is the world's only naturist golf course.

A 6-hole course near Bordeux, this nudist golf club also offers training courses and lessons but nudity is mandatory – weather permitting!

THE WORD "FORE!" ORIGINATED IN SCOTLAND AND IS A GOLFER'S WAY TO WARN OTHER PLAYERS ABOUT A WANDERING BALL. THE TERM IS MENTIONED AS FAR BACK AS 1881.

The odds of accidentally being hit by a golf ball are less than 1%.

A COMMON SUPERSTITION AMONG
GOLFERS IS TO NEVER WASH A BALL
IF THEY ARE HAVING A GREAT GAME.
IT IS BELIEVED THAT YOU WILL WASH
YOUR LUCK AWAY.

Another similar superstition is to never use a freshly washed ball to tee off - always wait at least one hole before using the ball you just washed!

515 YARDS IS THE LONGEST DRIVE EVER RECORDED AND WAS MADE BY MIKE AUSTIN, AN ENGLISH-AMERICAN PRO GOLFER, WHILE PLAYING IN THE U.S NATIONAL SENIORS TOURNAMENT IN 1974.

ALTHOUGH THE GUININESS WORLD BOOK OF RECORDS NO LONGER RECOGNISES IT AS THE WORLD'S LONGEST DRIVE IN THEIR BOOK, THE SHOT SECURED HIS NAME IN HISTORY.

Full name: Michael Hoke Austin

Born: February 17th 1910
Died: November 23rd 2005

Nickname: The Golfing Bandit - due to his hustles in his younger games making bets with vacationing gangsters at courses In South Florida.

A JAPANESE TRADITION IS THAT GOLFERS WHO GET A HOLE-IN-ONE ARE TO THROW A PARTY AND GIVE GIFTS, AS A WAY OF SHARING THEIR GOOD LUCK.

This tradition has led to many Japanese golfers buying insurance to protect themselves should their luck come in! For $65.00 a year the insurance covers party expenses of up to $3000.00. Almost 4 million Japanese amateur golfers have this insurance!

プ゚ セブン-イレブン
京都小川御池店
京都府京都市中京区小川通御池上ル
下古城町４００番
電話：075-251-6798    レジ#2

2013年08月08日(木) 00:06  責022

領 収 書

サントリー 天然水  550ML  ¥105
合  計        ¥105
お 預 り        ¥500
お  釣        ¥395
お買上明細は上記のとおりです。
商品価格には消費税等を含みます。

¥330,000

The Honourable Company of Edinburgh Golfers was the world's first golf club, founded in 1744.

Originating in Edinburgh, the town council annually gifted a silver club, for which the club played for.

The club is credited with drawing up the earliest written rules of the game, the 13 'Articles & Laws in Playing at Golf'.

RULES OF GOLF

H. C. E. G.

THE FIRST TIME THAT THE BRITISH OPEN WAS TELEVISED ON THE BBC WAS IN 1955.

THIS WAS HELD AT THE OLD COURSE AT ST. ANDREWS IN SCOTLAND, IN WHICH THE DEFENDING CHAMPION PETER THOMSON WON AGAIN.

The first ever golf tournament to be televised was in the U.S. This was the 1947 U.S Open, held at St. Louis Country Club and shown on the local network.

THE SHADOW CREEK GOLF COURSE IN LAS VEGAS IS THE MOST EXPENSIVE COURSE TO PLAY AT AROUND $500 FOR 18 HOLES.

OWNED BY CASINO MOGUL STEVE WYN, THE COURSE OPENED IN 1989 AND YOU MUST BE AN INVITED GUEST OF THE MGM MIRAGE RESORT IN ORDER TO PLAY. PLAYERS ARE EVEN DRIVEN TO AND FROM THE COURSE IN A LIMO!

Ireland has the third most expensive course in the world with Old Head Golf Links in Old Head of Kinsale, County Cork. The course costs around €375 per person, per round of golf.

AN 18-HOLE GAME OF GOLF CAN ALLOW YOU TO BURN MORE THAN 1400 CALORIES, WHICH IS THE SAME AS AN AVERAGE 30-MINUTE GYM SESSION.

FROM 1935 UP UNTIL THE CREATION OF THE MODERN GOLF BALL, MANY WOUND BALLS WERE FILLED WITH HONEY WITH A VULCANIZED LATEX COVER TO STOP THE BALL HAVING TOO MUCH SPIN.

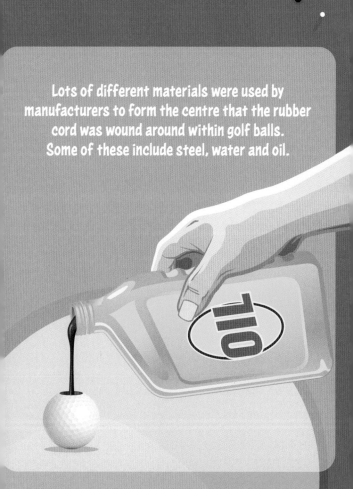

Lots of different materials were used by manufacturers to form the centre that the rubber cord was wound around within golf balls. Some of these include steel, water and oil.

AMERICANS SPEND OVER
600 MILLION DOLLARS ON GOLF
BALLS ALONE EVERY YEAR!

It's estimated that 1.2 billion balls are manufactured every year whilst a whopping 300 million balls are lost in the US alone. No wonder the spend on balls is so high!